A Box for Mits

By Debbie Croft

Mum had a big box.

"Mits! A box for you,"
said Tim.

Mits zips to the box.

Tim sets six bits on the mat.

"We can fix this!" said Mum.

"It is not a big job."

"A bit here," said Tim.

"Yes! And a bit here," said Mum.

Tap, tap!

"Sit, Mits," said Tim.
"You can not get in
the hut yet!"

"This bit can go up on top!" said Tim.

Mum hits the top bit.

Hit, hit.

"Not bad!" said Mum.

Mits sat in the hut.

CHECKING FOR MEANING

1. How many bits of the hut were in the box? *(Literal)*

2. What makes the *tap, tap* sound in the story? *(Literal)*

3. Why do you think Tim is building a hut for Mits? *(Inferential)*

EXTENDING VOCABULARY

yip	What does *yip* mean in this story? What makes this sound? What other sounds does Mits make?
six	What sounds are in the word *six*? What sound do the letters *ix* make? Can you find another word in the story that ends in –*ix*, but has a different letter at the start? What is the word?
yet	What does *yet* mean? What are the sounds in this word? If you change the first letter, what other words ending in –*et* can you make?

MOVING BEYOND THE TEXT

1. Have you ever helped to make something that came in a box? What was it? Was it a big job?

2. What do you think Mits will do in his new house?

3. Why do people get a special house for some pets?

4. What is Mum reading in the story? Why is this in the box with the pieces of the hut?

SPEED SOUNDS

Xx	Yy	Zz		
Kk	Ll	Vv	Qq	Ww
Dd	Jj	Oo	Gg	Uu
Cc	Bb	Rr	Ee	Ff	Hh	Nn
Mm	Ss	Aa	Pp	Ii	Tt

PRACTICE WORDS

zips

box

yip

fix

Yip

six

Yap

yet

Yes